GOD
WATCHES OVER US

GOD
WATCHES OVER US

My Living Testimonies

Leontine Birangui Mabika

Copyright © 2013, 2019 by Leontine Birangui Mabika.

ISBN Softcover   978-1-950580-68-2

All rights reserved. No part of this book may be reproduced or transmitted in any form or by any means, electronic or mechanical, including photocopying, recording, or by any information storage and retrieval system without express written permission from the author, except in the case of brief quotations embodied in critical reviews and certain other non-commercial uses permitted by copyright law.

Printed in the United States of America.

To order additional copies of this book, contact:
Bookwhip
1-855-339-3589
https://www.bookwhip.com

ACKNOWLEDGEMENT

I would like to sincerely thank our Father in heaven, Almighty God, for watching over me, guiding my life, and leading me to write this book to the glory of His name. My heartfelt appreciation for our four beautiful daughters—namely, Eunice, Diyenat, Maud, and Capucine—whom He has entrusted into our care. They are now adults, young professionals, ages twenty-seven to thirty-two years old. They have been loving, helpful, and very supportive. Capucine, under my dictation, typed the manuscript of this book.

I would like to express here my profound love and gratitude to my lovely and dear husband Pascal, who strengthened my faith in the Lord, from the first day he met me, and later on became my best friend until we got married. Without his patience, wisdom, support, and care for me and his daughters, writing this book would not have been possible.

I am also grateful for all those who have directly or indirectly contributed to the writing and publishing of this book especially my pastor and spiritual father, Charles Akwera and his spouse, Mama Muchungaji, Judith Akwera, to whom God has given a wonderful heritage: Glory, their daughter.

May our Almighty God bless you and reward you! May the purpose for which He had this book written be fulfilled! In Jesus' name I pray!

CONTENTS

Foreword 9

Introduction 13

The Various Stages of My Life 15

My Four Daughters 45

How God Has Transformed My Life 73

Conclusion 91

FOREWORD

The Bible says in 1 Chronicles 16:8–9,

> Give thanks unto the Lord, call upon His name, make known his deeds among the people.
> Sing unto him, sing psalms unto him, talk ye of all his wondrous works. (KJV)

It is in compliance with that scripture that I am writing this book to thank the Lord for my life and that of my family, especially for all His benefits and miracles since my childhood. The idea to write this book came to me a year ago, but I kept on procrastinating, finding excuses that I was too busy and that I would do it one day, until 2 October 2011 when I had a dream.

On 26 August 2011, my husband Pascal and I had traveled from Arusha, Tanzania, on home leave to Tours, France, and we were to return on 23 September 2011. A few weeks before traveling, I felt pains in my back and my legs were getting weak, which made walking difficult. I seized the opportunity of being in France to get the needed treatment. After several medical tests, I was told that a neurosurgery was required to remove a cyst that had grown in the lower part of my back due to a rough fall on my back five years ago while playing volleyball with my office teammates. The surgery took place on 26 September 2011, and I was discharged on the thirtieth. The neurosurgeon instructed me not to undertake any trip until after three weeks.

The night on 2 October until past midnight, I started falling asleep when I felt someone waking me up softly by touching my shoulder, while my husband was fast asleep beside me. I tried to open my eyes in the dark in an attempt to figure out what was happening. And I heard a voice telling me as in a reprimand, "You could have done something all the time you've been here. You could have written three books. It is not for nothing that I have extended your stay here!" As the voice spoke, I saw clearly the three books with titles, chapters, and some writings passed before my eyes, as well as how they would be written—one was by my husband in French and two by me in English. I woke up abruptly and woke up my husband to share that dream or vision. My husband was supportive; we prayed about it and decided to obey.

With that burden, I started to look the next morning for someone who could take dictation and type fast. This was how the first drafts of the two manuscripts were written: The first manuscript, which was dictated by my husband, was typed by a young Beninese who was introduced to us by my sister-in-law, Josephine. It was about his miraculous experience in Israel where he had fallen into a coma while we were on a vacation with our four daughters, and he was brought back to life with a message from the Lord. The second manuscript, under my dictation, was typed by my daughter Capucine who was then taking up an MBA at Liberty University in Virginia, USA. At that particular time, she had a few days off and wanted to visit us in France for six days. What a coincidence! The third and soon-to-be manuscript, given as a testimony in my church in Arusha, Tanzania, had already been recorded and will soon be typed and proofread.

The Lord was right! The job was done as He indicated and guided.

INTRODUCTION

I was born in Loubetsi, in the Republic of Congo—the capital city of which is Brazzaville—located in Central Africa. I am the fifth of a large family of twelve children—ten girls and two boys. My mom and dad were school teachers in a small village. I remember when I was five years old that I had a dream in which I saw a tall man coming and taking the hand of a small child and telling her, "Do not fear! I am God!" and I could see him walking with the small child and that child was me! This was my very first encounter with the Almighty God. I was raised in a Christian home. My mother was a daughter of a pastor. My grandfather, MBy Joseph, was the very first pastor of our district. He was trained by Swedish missionaries who were sent there for evangelization purposes. My mother and father used to attend his church services. He and his wife, MBoutsi Marie, loved us—their grandchildren—very much. They themselves had a family of nine. I remember as a kid, after the Sunday service, our grandfather would call me among others to go and count the offering in the church. I liked stacking the coins I collected from the offering baskets on top of each other. It was fun. I loved that task. It was from then I knew the offerings and tithes were part of the church service.

THE VARIOUS STAGES OF MY LIFE

IN CONGO-BRAZZAVILLE

I spent a wonderful childhood with my parents. I used to play a lot with my siblings. We all did domestic chores when required. I would see my mother cooking food for our large family, including the extended family—mainly the in-laws. In fact, I do not remember ever seeing the family living alone as mom, dad and children. We lived with many other relatives under the same roof.

I was very successful from primary school to the university level. I always came first; I was always the head and not the tail. While at University of Brazzaville, I joined a Christian group named *Cercle Biblique des Étudiants (CBE)*, which became later known as *Cercle Biblique Evangélique*. This was a youth group of the Evangelical Church of Congo. I enjoyed the fellowship there, singing for the Lord, and studying the

Word of God through Bible studies. We read and shared the gospel. It was a time of spiritual lifting. I got baptized in 1974 when I was twenty years old. It was within this group that I met my husband for the first time. He was a university student taking up sciences, especially chemistry, biology, and geology. Through a competitive examination in 1975, he obtained a scholarship to travel to France to further his studies. A year later, I also obtained a scholarship from the government to study languages and arts and went to France.

IN FRANCE

I obtained my first degree at the University of Lille III up to the doctorate level. I got married to my beloved husband and the Lord blessed us with four lovely daughters. We had set up a home in Lille, France. There, we met other countrymen who were also part of the CBE We met on a weekly basis at our house and prayed together. We also joined *L'Église Réformée de France*, a church in the city we were living in. Throughout my stay in France, I had two dreams that bothered me, and these were what I saw in my dreams:

DREAM ONE

We were on a highway with six lanes all going in one direction. They were occupied with the same type of car and there was only the driver in each one of them, no passengers. I was on the right hand side of the last lane. About forty meters away, there was a man sitting behind a desk facing the cars, and he was holding a big ledger. He beckoned to the drivers on the first row and asked them to step out of their cars and stand by its doors. Funny enough, every driver had a purse in his hand and its size would vary. I also came out of the car with my purse and it was the smallest of them all. He then called the first driver to move up to him. I could see the driver walking up to the man with the purse straight in his right hand for the man to see. The driver then sat behind the desk and had a conversation with him. After a few minutes, the driver stood up and went back to his car. Then the second driver was called and did the same. The third, the fourth, and the fifth, were also called, with the same routine. Then came my turn. I was feeling uncomfortable as I looked at my purse. I was wondering why it was that small. It should have been as big as the others or even bigger. I dragged my feet while approaching the man as if I feared to meet him. Finally, I reached there and sat behind the desk. He did not look at me, nor talked to me. The only thing he did was to let me read the ledger. I could see my name highlighted on one of the pages with a small dot next to it. I understood from that dot that my purse was too small. I then returned to my car having regrets about it. Just before getting inside my car, I woke up. The bible story of the talents then came back to my mind. I was convinced that the Lord was teaching me the importance of giving. That dream bothered me for a while. I then forgot it until I had my second dream.

DREAM TWO

It was a sunny day, and I was among those people who had gathered in a large room under a rectangular glass built structure. We were of various nationalities and races: blacks, whites, Asians, etc. People were busy laughing and talking, like in a stock exchange; some of them were even dancing. There was no one outside the room, not even a single animal. I was in the front row, near the right corner, and was busy cooking; my sisters were in the left corner and indeed, there was life in the room. When I looked up, I was surprised to see a man walking up toward the room. I asked myself, "What is that man doing out there alone?" Before I could even come up with an answer, the man walked through the glass and stood right next to me. I wondered how he could possibly do that. While I was maybe washing the dishes, I cannot remember exactly, he then said to me, "Where do you think these people are going?" I looked at him and then followed the direction of his eyes. I saw a Challenger-type spacecraft with passengers inside traveling to the moon. I responded, "They are going to the moon!" He laughed. I was surprised to see him laughing, as if he was minimizing that fact. He then said to me, "If I want, I can stop them." I also laughed and went back to what I was doing, as if not paying enough attention. Then the man said again, "If I want, I can stop all this noise." I glanced at him skeptically and said to myself, "Who does he think he is?" Then he said, "Hmmm, when I speak, nobody listens!" There were large speakers at every corner in the room. The next thing I saw was that he put his right hand on top of the speaker that was in our corner, and as he did that, a sudden general power outage followed. All the noise stopped short. Everyone was surprised and was wondering what had happened. They all screamed, "Ahhhhh!" as if in disagreement. Then he moved away from me, walked across the room, and stood facing all of us in the middle of the back wall, at a door that none of us saw. He did not say anything else. Somehow, we all understood that each one of us had to go and speak to him. Two lines were automatically formed; however, some people began to panic as they looked for their families and friends. Afraid and in tears, I also searched for my sisters, my friends, and my children, wondering what was going to happen. I did not find any of them, so I ended lining up. There was a long queue in front of me. I could see people in front talking to the man one by one, and then he would either point to the right or to the left as to where they would go. None of them returned to tell us what happened. When my turn was approaching, I was so afraid that I would let the person behind me go first, and I did this twice. My turn eventually came. I remember being heavily pregnant, and out of nowhere, Eunice and Diyenat were running toward me, then held both my hands, Eunice on my right and Diyenat on my left. They were maybe two and four years old. I could not look directly at the man's face, but I could feel a sense of peace in him touching my heart. His look upon me felt like eternity, as if he was searching for something inside my soul. I felt ashamed. I knew deep down in my heart that I wasn't ready to face him. I had not done what the man had wanted me to do and that I had failed. I kept my head down. Surprisingly, he said, "Okay, it's all right! You can move to the right hand side." I was somehow convinced that it was the right side to go to, and I felt the divine grace because I knew that I did not deserve to go in that direction. Just before I started heading to the right, I said to him with my head still bowed, "Can I take my children with me?" He said, "Yes, you may take them with you." I lifted my two daughters in my arms and walked not very far. At that particular moment, I remembered that my husband was still queuing, so I stopped and asked him again, "Can I take my husband also with me?" He responded with a strong and authoritative voice, "No, his turn will come, just get your daughters and go!" I walked away sadly with tears on my face. I could feel he was staring back at me.

"When you wake up, tell them this is exactly what's going to happen!" he said.

"Who would believe me? Would anyone even believe me?" I responded without looking back.

I felt anxious and nervous; I rubbed my hands. The next thing I remembered was my husband trying to wake me up in the middle of the night because I had been crying in my sleep. I was still saying to myself, "Who would believe me?" Feeling confused, my husband responded, "Who would believe what?" My pillow was completely wet due to my tears. Then I told my husband the dream I just had.

In 1987, a year before finishing my Ph.D, I miraculously got a job after many unsuccessful attempts. There was an advertisement in the newspaper that an African institution was looking for a translator. I immediately applied for the position and was later called for an interview. I left my newborn baby in the care of my husband as I had to go and sit for an exam in the Bank of Central African States (*Banque des États de l'Afrique Centrale or BEAC*) in Yaoundé, Cameroon. I remember there was one guy on the interview panel—who never knew me or had seen me before—who was very positive about my performance and was defending my case against the other three whom he doubted. I went back to France and continued to pray. One day, I got a phone call from the head of the regional office of the Bank of Central African States requesting me to travel to Paris for another written test for the same vacancy. I took that test. After two long months, I received a letter breaking the great news to me that I had passed. I was going to be recruited by the African Centre for Monetary Studies based in Dakar, Senegal. I would be on probation for six months and would then be recruited on a permanent basis and enjoy the relevant benefits for my family and myself. My husband stayed in Lille, France, with our four daughters for six months. They were six, four, three years old, and the last born at six months.

At this juncture, I would like to thank God for my husband who took good care of our young children while I was attending university. He did a tremendous job for which I am deeply proud and grateful to him and our Almighty God. By the time the family joined me in Dakar six months later, my children could not recognize me, especially the youngest. They had grown close to their father. I remember, while living together, whenever my daughters wanted anything, even food, they would first turn to their father, before realizing I was also there and that I could also help. I praise God for such a bond between my daughters and their father.

IN DAKAR, SENEGAL

I am very grateful to God for that very first international job at the African Centre for Monetary Studies (ACMS). I had tried before to get into the African Development Bank based in *Côte d'Ivoire* and into the International Monetary Fund in Washington, DC, but was unsuccessful. At the ACMS, I traveled extensively and acquired work experience as a translator-interpreter. At the same time, I was the head of the secretarial pool of the ACMS. I also gained my first experience as a supervisor. I performed tremendously well to the satisfaction of the management. I remember one day I was sick and I could not go to the office. I informed my immediate supervisor who then told the director general of the ACMS. The latter made the following comment, "Mrs. Mabika is sick today? This must be true because I know she would not lie." When I heard this remark, I thanked God for the image and integrity that I unknowingly portrayed while working there.

As part of the benefits of that institution, I would travel home to Congo-Brazzaville every other year on home leave with my whole family. This gave our children the unique opportunity to touch base with their relatives as they were all born in France.

Despite Senegal being a Muslim country, my husband and I joined the only protestant church in Dakar. It was called *Eglise Protestante du Sénégal*. The pastor was the son of the only Senegalese protestant family at the time. We became actively involved in the service groups of the church. I was the head of the Sunday school and the head of the women's group. My husband was the head of the youth group because of his experience in the youth ministry of our home church in Congo-Brazzaville, the *Eglise Evangélique du Congo*. Later on, my husband was elected as the youngest member of the Board of Elders in the *Eglise Protestante* in addition to belonging to the service group in charge of the building and maintenance of the church property given his architectural background.

Our children grew physically and also spiritually in Senegal. We taught them how to read the word, pray, and worship. And we were able to see the fruits of their spiritual growth when we moved back to France six years later after the African Centre for Monetary Studies closed down for restructuring. We packed and sent all our personal belongings to Congo-Brazzaville, our home country, where we believed to return soon. Unfortunately, civil war broke out in Congo in 1993. There were mass killings, looting, and displacement of persons. This lasted for a couple of years. I lost family members, belongings, and real estate property, as well as the family house where I grew up with my parents and siblings. My mother, my late young brother Parfait and his son Eddy, and aunts were among those displaced. They walked long distances in the forest to run away from the killings and found refuge in the neighboring countries, mostly in Gabon. Here again, I would like to extend my deep appreciation to our heavenly Father for having protected, in His faithfulness, my relatives during those hard times of survival. I was able to see them again many years later, although in very poor health condition. Needless to say, thousands of people lost their lives under those circumstances.

When I had to leave the ACMS like all the other staff, my husband took our four daughters back to Lille, France, while I stayed behind for another three months to take care of the administrative duties. I joined them later in Lille where we resettled and my children resumed their schooling. A few days later, I received a phone call from my younger sister Rose, in the United States—a twin who was married to an American with two children. She was working as a program officer for the United Nations Development Fund for Women (UNIFEM). In our conversation, I mentioned to her that I had just returned from Senegal and that I was looking for another employment. She advised me to contact some international organizations for the possibility of doing some translations for them as a freelance translator and to find time to visit her in the United States of America. With my husband's consent, I traveled to the US for the first time. My husband and children stayed in France.

IN THE UNITED STATES OF AMERICA

I followed my sister's advice. I took my resume and credentials and wrote many letters to different organizations worldwide, including the World Bank and the International Monetary Fund. I then traveled to America. I first went to New York and stayed with my sister in New Jersey for two months. In December 1993, my husband and children joined us for Christmas. It was also their first time to visit America. We spent a wonderful Christmas together. When they went back to France in January 1994, I decided to travel to Washington, DC, to visit our embassy and possibly follow up on the letters I had sent to the World Bank and the International Monetary Fund. I took the Greyhound bus at midnight from Port Authority, NY to Washington, DC bus terminal and arrived there at 4:30 a.m. I waited at the bus stop until 6:00 a.m. Then I took a taxi to my hotel where I had booked a room not far from K Street.

The next morning, I went to the World Bank Group and the International Monetary Fund to check if they had received my letters. I also went to the Embassy of the Republic of Congo to introduce myself and greet my countrymen. Then I returned to France to follow up on some of my applications there. A few weeks later, I was called by a World Bank senior official for a short-term consultant contract which consisted of editing and proofreading documents of the World Bank's Economic Development Institute. The assignment was to be done at home. Then another consultant contract came from UNIFEM as an interpreter for some of their meetings outside the US. Later on, I received a phone call from the Embassy of the Republic of Congo, inviting me to travel back to Washington, DC, to meet the newly appointed ambassador. They explained to me that the embassy would need my services as a translator and interpreter, as the ambassador could not speak English and was at that time alone; the other Congolese officials were to join him at a later stage. God's favor was upon me and I acknowledged Him again for opening the doors before me.

When I came back, I stayed at the same hotel for one month. The embassy processed my work papers with the Congolese government in Brazzaville and with the US Embassy in Paris. Then I started my work at the embassy. I assisted the ambassador in his meetings at the US Department of State, with international organizations, and wrote all the reports for the benefit of the Congolese government. I also did some pro bono translation jobs for the Group of African Ambassadors in Washington, DC. While the ambassador was away, I also supervised the embassy's personnel including his two local secretaries and one clerk.

While I was living in the hotel, there was an incident that occurred which is worth mentioning. At night, I would usually go to sleep after locking the door in my room, but I never thought of putting on its chain. One night, just before sleeping, I prayed and laid my head on the pillow. The Holy Spirit spoke to me and said, "Why don't you put the chain of the door on?" I got up and quickly put it on. Very early the next morning, I woke up and started to get ready for work. When I looked at the door, I could not believe my eyes. The door was unlocked and slightly open, but the chain was still on. I realized with horror that someone had tried to break quietly into my room, probably using a master key, but failed to do so because of the chain. Although I am a light sleeper, I did not hear any noise. I was grateful to God for having warned me moments before. He had thus preserved my life that night. I am also grateful that I was able to obey the Spirit!

SILVER SPRING, MARYLAND

I eventually moved into an apartment in Silver Spring, Maryland, to facilitate family visits from France. My family visited me twice a year whenever school was closed for summer or during Christmas time. And I enjoyed receiving letters from my family, especially my daughters. One example is Maud's letter.

> Villeneuve d'Ascq
> le 17 février 96
>
> Chère maman,
>
> Tout se passe très bien à la maison. Je t'écris avec la machine à écrire que nous avons achetée à mon test d'anglais, j'ai eu 51/60 C'est Sarah Naïs qui a eu la meilleure note. J'ai augmenté en sciences naturelles, j'ai maintenant 15,5 de moyenne. Je prie toujours pour la personne pour qui je dois prier mais cient'à encore changer. Papa nous a dit qu'il faut économiser de l'argent pour aller au Congo ou soit aux Etats-Unis. Mais moi je préfère aller au Congo parce que ça fait longtemps que nous avons vu la famille au Congo.
>
> Est-ce que tu viendras avec nous au Congo ou aux Etats-Unis? J'espère que tu viendras avec nous. Je m'occupe beaucoup de Capucine et elle commence à respecter les plus grandes qu'elle. Je m'améliore beaucoup au piano et quand tu viendras à la maison, je te jouerai un morceau. Nous prions tous pour que nous nous retrouverons un jour tous ensemble dans le nouvel appartement de Washington.
>
> Que Dieu te garde !
>
> Ta fille chérie Maud
> Signature:
>
> P.S. Je t'écrirai plus souvent !

After moving in, I started looking for a local Christian church. Some people advised me to try the many churches along Sixteenth Street, but I did not feel comfortable with that. I let God and trusted Him to direct me to the right church where He wanted me to serve, and I prayed for several weeks. One day, I had to represent the embassy at a meeting in the US Department of State with other diplomatic missions. The meeting lasted the whole day. At the end, the participants exchanged business cards. I received business cards from my counterparts. One official from an African embassy introduced himself to me and gave me a card of his church instead of his business card. I was pleasantly surprised for that was not the place one would expect to be presented with such a card. The card read "Bethel World Outreach Ministries." I quickly realized in my heart that this was the answer to my prayers. I inquired from this official where that church was. He gave me the direction and indicated that he would be ready to pick me up from Silver Spring Metro station the next day as there was an evening service. That was how I attended the church service at Bethel World Outreach Ministries for the first time. The church happened to be located right behind my new apartment. During the service, I felt welcomed and comfortable. I could feel that this was the church I was going to be part of. At the end of the church service, there was an announcement that the church was looking for interpreters to translate the sermons of the pastor from English into French as many French-speaking people who could not understand English were attending the church services. Being an interpreter, I felt as if that appeal was specifically addressed to me—an opportunity for me to serve. I had the conviction right there that this was the local church God had given me. I introduced myself to the church leaders and volunteered to serve in that area. I became a member of Bethel World Outreach Ministries and served there faithfully as an interpreter. I quickly grew spiritually attending home cell meetings and other fellowships of Bethel. I met many people—brothers and sisters in Christ—and made friends. I was very happy with the Christian community God had brought me into. When my husband and children visited me, we went to Bethel together. My daughters introduced themselves and were given an opportunity to show what they could do for the Lord. They played the flute and sang the songs they had written themselves. I praised the Lord, for later on, whenever they came to the US, they would be asked to play music at our home cell fellowship.

At the embassy, we started facing financial challenges, as the funds expected from the central government to smoothly run its operations were not forthcoming. As a result, the staff members were not receiving their salaries as regularly as desirable. We could work for three to six months without income. Bills started piling up, and I could no longer afford my rent. I had to resort to doing private translations at home to make ends meet. I would work during the day at the embassy, and at night, work from home, translating documents till early mornings. I remember one night being so tired from working late on a document to be handed in the next morning. I was dozing on my computer in the middle of the night when I heard a soft voice calling my name, "Leontine! Leontine!" While I was slowly awakened by it, I responded, "Hein!" and then regained my strength to complete the job and sent it just in time via email. I earned some money to pay my rent. I also remember an incident that occurred in my apartment during that period. My apartment was located on the tenth floor. I had slept very late—in the early morning of a Saturday—after working on my translations. I was fast asleep. I was awakened abruptly by a voice saying, "Leontine, wake up! Don't you know there is fire?" I sat up and repeated, as if wondering whether I heard it well, "Fire?" Instinctively, I got out of bed and ran out of my bedroom, and then out of the apartment. Strangely, my corridor was very quiet and there was no one to be seen. I started running down the staircases in panic. I became concerned, especially when I did not see or meet anyone on the way. Then I began to wonder whether I was in a dream or in the real world. When I reached down and came out, I was shocked to see a large crowd outside and firefighters were busy putting out the fire on one of the floors below mine. Some of them who saw me came out murmured in amazement as if to say there was still someone inside. I was breathless and then one security officer ran to me and quickly moved me away from the scene. I was then told of the story that the fire had started on the fifth floor. The fire alarm was rung for over fifteen minutes to evacuate the building and I did not hear it in my sleep. It was around 11:00 a.m. It was then that I realized I was still in my pajamas and that the Holy Spirit had saved me from danger. I was grateful that the Lord was watching over me.

At the church, there was a call for pledges to buy a building—the building where we held our meetings for church services. Like many other members of the congregation, I pledged $1,000 to be redeemed over a year. I believed God for a breakthrough. At the same time, I would go to work at the embassy and still work for the whole day, although I was not sure if I would receive my remuneration any time soon. Every time I would be blessed with one translation to do, I would take part of the corresponding fees and give it to the church to fulfill my pledge. As the situation at the embassy deteriorated, the ambassador took a trip to the home country to consult the relevant authorities.

One morning, while supervising the day-to-day operations of the embassy in the absence of the ambassador, I received a phone call from the ambassador of Mali. He said that he would need my services as an interpreter for a Malian high official who had come to Washington, DC, for official business and being a French speaker. The two of us accompanied the official to all his meetings held in DC, and I did the translation for him on a pro bono basis, as was usually the case whenever an African embassy requested my assistance in that area; his visit lasted one day. At the end of the day, this man—who was actually the Special Representative of the Secretary General (SRSG) in the United Nations Angola Verification Mission in Luanda, Angola—left after thanking the ambassador of Mali and I for our assistance and gave us his business card.

He added that if one day we were looking for another job opportunity, we might want to write to the UN Headquarters (UNHQ) in New York. "You never know," he said. I followed his advice. I sent my resume to the UN Headquarters and continued to work at the embassy. The ambassador stayed in the home country longer than expected. One day, he called me on the phone to inform me that he was not coming back because he had been given a new assignment. He instructed me to break the news to the staff and let them go. This came as a shock to me and to my other colleagues.

GOD'S HAND

One evening, while I was in the process of implementing the ambassador's instruction, I received a phone call from an official at the UN Headquarters, asking me to travel there with my resume. I quickly booked an appointment and traveled to New York. There, I stayed with my sister Rose in Secaucus, New Jersey. The next morning, I went to the UN Headquarters and was welcomed on the ground floor by the secretary of the chief for the Department of Peacekeeping Operations and was taken upstairs. It was my first time entering the United Nations building, and I was impressed by its height.

The secretary took me to a small office where I filled out a form with information relating to personal status, educational and professional experience. She said, "While waiting for my boss who is in a meeting, kindly fill in this UN profile form called P11. I'll return when he's ready to see you." After an hour or so, she came to take me to the UN official I was to meet. The said official was the chief and he had already read my resume and found it interesting. He asked me to hand over to him the P11 and started reading it. Then he interviewed me. An hour later, he picked up his phone and called someone into his office. When a young man came in, he said to him, "Please take Ms. Mabika to the travel department; we're giving her an SSA (Special Service Agreement) for Angola to work at our peacekeeping mission there in Luanda as an interpreter for three months." I had to confess that I did not really understand his jargon, but I guessed I was being offered a short-term contract. My heart started beating fast. I could not believe my ears. I was jumping with joy in my heart and in my mind.

"She's not sitting for the written test then?" the young man asked.

"There's no need," the chief answered, and then continued, "because she has already translated for the Special Representative of the Secretary General in Washington, DC, for a whole day and it was satisfactory, I have been informed."

The young man asked me to follow him. I was thanking God all the way from the contract department where I signed the SSA to the travel department where I got my business class ticket to fly to Angola. All this was so overwhelming. The favor of God over my situation was unspeakable. By the time

I came out of the UN Headquarters, it was already 5:00 p.m., but I had with me a three-month contract, an air ticket, and a form I had to take to my doctor for checkup and issuance of a medical certificate in order to complete my file at the contract department.

Once outside, I called my husband in France to tell him the miracle the Lord had done. Not only the Lord had provided me with a unique employment, but also had given me a free ticket to travel to Angola, with a stopover in Paris for transit to enable me to see my family and bid them farewell. I showed my sister Rose and my mother, who was also visiting from Congo-Brazzaville, everything I had been given and related to them the story. They found it hard to believe. Rose commented that she knew a number of people who had, over the years, applied for positions at the UN Headquarters, including herself, but had not succeeded. Most of them have not even received any response with their applications, and how come that in one day I was able to access the UN building and came out with a contract and an air ticket to travel within a week. It was God! It is only my Father who is able to perform such a miracle! Thank you Father!

My mother was keen on helping me pack and I also wanted her to see DC, so the next day we took the Greyhound bus to Washington, DC. There, we went to church for the first time and shared my testimony. The bishop talked about me before the congregation and in these encouraging words he said,

"Leontine is among the very few members who have paid up their pledges for the purchase of the church building, and I am not surprised that God has opened this big door for her." He prayed for me and the whole church bid me farewell at a small party. I told them that I was leaving only for a few months and that I would be back soon. I then flew to Paris to see my husband and my children and shared with them the miracle before taking my connecting flight to Angola.

IN ANGOLA

I arrived in Luanda, Angola on 3 October 1995. The duty station was called the United Nations Angola Verification Mission III (UNAVEM III). It was a non-family duty station, the largest UN peacekeeping mission at that time with about ten thousand troops.

The staff was working and living in containers in a specific area away from the city center. It was a camp reserved for the UN troops and civilian staff. As UN personnel, we were not allowed to go to the city center, nor stay late outside. It was too dangerous.

I joined a dynamic team of interpreters and translators in the Language Section on the mission field in Luanda, the headquarters. The working languages of the mission were English, French, and Portuguese. I was assigned to the office of the head of the mission, the Special Representative of the

Secretary General (SRSG), who was a French-speaker from Mali. I also joined a newly established Christian fellowship which initially had five members. The fellowship quickly increased in numbers. We had our church services within the mission compound. The services and prayer sessions were led by spiritually mature Christians. We had no substantive pastor.

Life in the mission was not ordinary. We lived in containers that were arranged and furnished by the management of UNAVEM III. You would be assigned to a container on a first-come, first-served basis. As a result, you had no possibility of choosing your roommate(s). You would end up living with people you did not know at all. A lot of patience was needed to cope with people that you shared your container with—some with odd habits and sometimes of the opposite gender. It was not easy. The good thing was that we worked in a multicultural setting which was very interesting. Once you survive in such an environment, you could practically work anywhere. You get exposed to people of various races, of different nationalities and backgrounds. It constituted a challenge to take up, but also could become an asset.

At first, I had to live in a hotel for almost three months while waiting for a free space in one of the containers available. It was paid by the peacekeeping mission. During that time, I prayed earnestly to God that He would give me a Christian roommate who did not drink or smoke like myself. The Lord proved himself faithful once again. One day, the administration called and assigned me a brand new two-room container. I stayed alone for a few days before a young black American lady was sent to stay with me. She was not a churchgoer, so to speak, but was an easygoing and respectful person. I was so thankful to the Lord. I had peace of mind. She stayed with me for a month and a half and then was sent to one of the regional offices in the Angolan territory.

During my three-month service period, I worked closely with the SRSG as one of his three interpreters. I covered the closed meetings of the SRSG with high officials of the government of Angola, the UN senior officials who visited UNAVEM III, the heads of international organizations and diplomatic missions, and other government representatives, who played vital roles in nation building and in the restoration of peace in Angola.

Angola was then torn by thirteen years of civil war between two warring parties: the MPLA led by President Dos Santos and UNITA led by the late Jonas Savimbi. The mandate of the United Nations peacekeeping mission in Angola was to bring the warring parties to the table of negotiations and reach an agreement in stopping the devastating conflict and setting up a government of national reconciliation and peace.

In the course of my duties in the office of the SRSG, I had the opportunity to travel, meet and translate for many dignitaries on the occasion of their visits to the mission or outside the mission area. These were, among others, African Head of States such as His Excellency Nelson Mandela of South Africa; the UN Secretary General, His Excellency Kofi Annan; the Managing Director of the International Monetary Fund, His Excellency Michel Camdessus; and the US Secretary of State, Her Excellency Madeleine Albright. During that mission time, I almost had no contact with the outside world. As my prayer time increased, I developed a close relationship with God, and my fellowship with Him intensified. I also developed the habit of staying quiet before the Lord after every prayer to hear from Him. And the Lord would speak to me and I would quickly write those messages down on a notebook. I would like here to reiterate my appreciation to my Father, the Almighty God, for the quiet time I spent in His presence and the revelations He gave me during that time concerning my husband and our four daughters, which came to pass years later.

I remember a specific incident when my three-month contract had expired and I prayed to God that I would be given an extension of the said contract. One day, the chief of personnel informed me that I should start packing to leave the mission. He said, "Your contract is not going to be extended because you did not perform well according to the SRSG." That same night, I went before the Lord and cried out to Him saying, "Lord, for the past three months, I believe, I worked to the best of my ability. They say, the SRSG, the head of the mission, is not satisfied with my performance. I had started gaining international experience. Where then are you taking me Lord?" The next day, I started the check-out process. I went to the office of the SRSG and requested his special advisor to sign me out before doing the same thing with the other sections of the mission. He was surprised to hear that I had to leave the mission. He told me to sit down in his office for a minute and quickly went out to see the SRSG to seek confirmation of that fact. When he came back, he told me that the SRSG would like to see me. I immediately headed to the SRSG's office. I was pleasantly surprised to hear from his own mouth that he had never told anybody that he was not satisfied with my work, nor has he ever talked to the chief of personnel about such a thing. He could not therefore understand why I was told to leave the mission since he had personally requested from him the renewal of the contracts of all the interpreters. I was later on informed that he spoke to the Deputy SRSG and asked him to sort out that issue with the administration. That same day, the chief of personnel came to my office and apologized for the misunderstanding and the confusion it created, and he also indicated that my contract would be renewed. I found out, afterwards, that someone had wanted to replace me with one of his friends. I rendered my heartfelt gratitude to the Lord Jesus Christ for being my warrior, fighting for my sake and giving me victory, right there and then. I was so grateful for His powerful intervention.

When my contract was extended, my status in the mission changed. I became a UN staff member with a contract renewable every six months as every other civilian staff on the mission field. I could then enjoy all the benefits associated with a staff member status, which was not the case when I only had the SSA (Special Service Agreement). The new contract gave me the right to family visits as I was in a non-family duty station. I could therefore travel to France for a week every three months during my CTO (Compensatory Time Off) or my RNR (Rest and Recuperation) to visit my husband and children. I remember the time I took the trip to France to visit my family; it was a moment of excitement and joy. We were reunited after nine months on the mission area. They had prepared a small party to welcome me home, and on that occasion, I not only received gifts from my children, but also another surprise in the form of a song that they had written and played with musical instruments; Maud was on the piano, Capucine, Diyenat and Eunice played the flute. they sang it together. The lyrics of the song translated from French read as follows: "Mom, we love you. We love you because you are our mother. Even when you are not with us, we will always love you." I was deeply moved by that song. It touched my heart so much and I have never forgotten it. I would find myself singing it from time to time. I was the happiest mother ever. My eyes were filled with tears of joy. How thoughtful of them!

God has blessed me with a wonderful husband who can also play the guitar, and he would do so along with our beautiful and loving children. I would start singing a chorus that all of us knew while they played their instruments. It would be a nice worship time before the Lord. As a family, we could form a little band. I would like here to commend my husband for having allowed me to go and work away from the family and, during that time, for patiently teaching our daughters many things such as cooking, washing dishes, ironing, shopping, cleaning, being ladies, playing instruments, praying and serving God. I am so grateful to God for such a family! My husband described the time he spent with his daughters in more detail in the book he wrote entitled *Twelve Days in Coma*.

In 1996, I used one of my rest-and-recuperation periods to travel to Congo-Brazzaville where I was to meet my family in order to visit our relatives together. Our children not only had the opportunity to interact with the Congolese extended family but also to familiarize themselves with the Congolese culture and customs. I would like at this juncture to thank again my heavenly Father for having divinely planned this trip. Civil war broke out in Congo shortly after we left.

MY FOUR DAUGHTERS

Throughout my stay in the mission area in Angola, my fellowship with the Lord grew considerably. I became very sensitive to the promptings of the Holy Spirit and to the voice of the Lord. I would like to highlight here some of the specific messages that the Lord had given me about my daughters during my prayer time with him. I had recorded and shared the said messages with them.

Concerning my firstborn, Eunice, aged thirty-one, she had a slight hearing problem in one ear. The Lord had indicated to me one day that He would heal that ear and that she would become a woman of faith. As for my second born, Diyenat, aged twenty-nine, the Lord had said that she would be a mother to many children and that He would give her the heart of a mother. For my third daughter, Maud, aged twenty-eight, the Lord had revealed to me that she would continue to play the piano and would be praising Him in concerts and churches. And for my last born, Capucine, aged twenty-six, the Lord had revealed to me that He has endowed her with a healing power in her hands and that she would be able to pray for people so that they would be healed.

At the time of writing, the Lord had already fulfilled His promises in my daughters' lives. Eunice was selected among many—after seven interviews—for a dream job with an international organization in Washington, DC, as an associate investment officer immediately after her MBA because of her faith in God. God had spoken to us as a family on several occasions through revelations He made to Eunice. Diyenat loves taking care of young children, whether at Sunday school or in any other environment. She loves nurturing them and the children love her, too. We could see young children visit our home to look for her. Currently, she is working in Arusha and is very much involved in helping an orphanage. She also loves to take care of puppies. Maud had worked in Connecticut. She was the leader of a young adult praise and worship team. She played the piano for the church music ministry and was the only female pianist of a worship band; they organized concerts for evangelization purposes in a number of places in America. She has ministered to many people in the Kingdom of God. Maud has moved to Washington, DC, for a miracle job offer with a promotion she received from a long-standing firm in DC. She is the leader of the youth band in her church in D.C. Capucine was the youngest captain of the school basketball team for four consecutive years and given the nickname "Cap" (short for Captain or Capucine) while she was boarding in the

American School in Switzerland (TASIS). She obtained her bachelor's degree and her masters at Liberty University—a Christian university in Lynchburg, Virginia. She was a prayer leader and also the leader of their dance team there. In those capacities, God had given her many opportunities to speak with, counsel and pray for her classmates or teammates, and healings whether spiritual or physical had taken place. During the first week of November 2012, she just had an encounter with God while she was praying in a dream, and I would leave my daughter to relate that herself.

I would like once again to recognize and appreciate God's faithfulness in my life and that of my family. How awesome He has been!

Another unforgettable experience that I had while in Angola was the following: I had worked on the mission field for about two years. In 1997, upon my return from a family visit in France, I received a fax which came from the peacekeeping department in New York making an offer to me. They wanted to know if I was willing to move to the newly established UN International Criminal Tribunal for Rwanda (UNICTR) based in Arusha, Tanzania, but with an office in Kigali, Rwanda. The tribunal was in need of interpreters and translators, and I was being offered a one-year contract at the same level as I had in Angola, which was a P2 (Professional category, level II). The working conditions and the entitlements were different from those in Angola. So, I debated for a while to find out whether I should accept it or not. I weighed the pros and the cons of both positions. In most cases, whenever one was offered a contract to take up a new position elsewhere, it would come with a promotion. This was not the case with the offer I received. The UNICTR in Kigali was a family duty station and was giving a longer contract on a fixed-term basis. However, the working environment was not as rewarding as the one I had at UNAVEM where I was attached to the office of the head of the mission. I spoke with my immediate supervisor and the SRSG for advice and they both were not really in favor of the offer, especially since Rwanda had just experienced genocide and life would be pretty difficult there. Furthermore, there was no promotion associated with the move. My fellow Christians prayed for me. They were also of the view that I would be better off here than in Rwanda, quoting the saying "The devil you know is better than the one you don't know." I was in a dilemma. I went to my heavenly Father in prayer and fasting.

One night, after I prayed to the Lord, I remained silent in His presence, ready to hear from Him. An inner voice spoke and said, "Just follow my footsteps." I could picture in my mind that I was walking before the Lord, I thus followed Him, putting my own steps right in His footprints. I clearly understood that I had to move with God and I had peace with it. I shared this revelation with my husband, and we agreed that I should move. I therefore accepted the offer. I broke the news to the SRSG, my supervisor and my colleagues, as well as my fellow Christians. I told them I had made up my mind and that I would go to Rwanda. No one really understood that decision as it ran against the general view and feelings of others. However, they organized separate befitting farewell parties for me—one was by the SRSG and his office; the second by the Language Section; the third by my friends; and the fourth by my brothers and sisters in Christ. I flew out of Angola with peace in my heart, trusting God for my future. I first traveled to France to visit my family. I stayed with them for two weeks and spent quality time with them before heading for Rwanda, Kigali, to take up the job with the United Nations International Criminal Tribunal for Rwanda.

IN RWANDA

I arrived in Rwanda in the evening of June 9, 1997, on board a Sabena flight. I was put in Umubano Hotel as private accommodation was scarce and difficult to come by. I stayed in that hotel for one month.

I joined the Language Section of the ICTR; its office was based in Rwanda. The ICTR headquarters was located in Arusha, Tanzania. I met my fellow translators-interpreters. Given my professional experience, my performance quickly became noticeable. I would be sent here and there by the head of the Language Section, to cover the meetings of ICTR management with the staff, those of the investigators and the lawyers, as well as meetings with other UN agencies based in Kigali.

While complying with the administrative procedure at the personnel section, I happened to know that I was the only translator-interpreter at the P2 level; almost all my colleagues had joined at the P3 level. I started my work. I worked with all my heart. I thank God my performance was highly appreciated in the workplace. As time went by, I submitted a letter of appeal to the UN Headquarters through the ICTR management, requesting for a review of my entry level.

In the meantime, I joined a local church called Shining Light Church. There, I had the opportunity to serve in the praise and worship team, and then later on learned how to lead them in English. The leader at that time was a colleague of mine, who also worked as a translator at the ICTR. I used to call her Sister Lola. She helped and encouraged me to take my first step in the noble service of praise and worship. May the Lord bless her! We became friends. A year later, the pastor of the church died and his spiritual father, Pastor Dan, came from Dar es Salaam for the funeral. He encouraged the wife of the late pastor and the church members not to lose heart and to continue with the work of the Lord. The widow felt a call from God to take over the church and minister to the members. It was in that young church that I also met some of my colleagues from ICTR who, later on, became very good friends and brethren in Christ—namely, the late Sister Olamide, Ayo and Bayo, and Pastors Evelyn and Randolph Tebbs.

All of us continued to serve God in Shining Light Church and supported Pastor Jolly who became our new pastor. The church started growing. We became elders of the church and ministered in various capacities. I started leading the praise and worship in the church and then put in place a choir. By that time, upon Sister Olamide's invitation, I had moved out of the Umubano Hotel into the apartment jointly rented by her, Ayo and Bayo, while still looking for a place of my own. I eventually found a five-bedroom house, keeping in mind the size of my family. The rent was very high, about $2,000 a month, due to the fact that Kigali had just come out of genocide, and there were no more houses or apartments available, so I took it. I had to pay a three-month deposit before moving in, but I had no money as I was not yet on the UN payroll—a process that could take up to six months. I prayed that God would provide for me financially. HR (Human Resources) informed me that I could request for a salary advance, but that the process could also take a number of weeks to go through. I shared my predicament with one of my colleague interpreters, a French citizen, whom I had known only for a month. He voluntarily offered to give me the $6,000 needed for the deposit on the spot, without thinking twice. I appreciated him wholeheartedly for his trust. He did not even ask me when I would be able to refund him. I saw here again the gracious hand of God moving in my favor. I was then able to pay the deposit required and a receipt for that amount was issued, which I was to submit to the office to support my salary advance request.

GOD'S MIRACLES

A very strange thing happened. On the day I was to take the receipt to HR, I looked for it in my bag but I could not find it. I searched everywhere—in between documents, in my office, and in the small room that I was occupying. No receipt. I became concerned for I could not believe I had lost the receipt that was given to me just a few days before. I called my roommates to help me search in the apartment, just in case, but still nothing. I wondered where I had misplaced it. That night, I prayed earnestly to God asking Him to show me where I had put that receipt. As I woke up the next morning, the very first thing I saw was an envelope placed conspicuously on the small coffee table I was using as a desk, as if to make sure I would see it as soon as I get up. I got out of my bed, curious and wondering what that was. I reached out to grab the envelope and opened it. There was the receipt I was looking for! I almost screamed. I left the envelope leaning against a book and ran out to call my roommates to inform them that the receipt was found. They rushed into my room and they were as bewildered as I was of what had happened. Up to today, I did not know who brought it. The only thing I am convinced of and grateful for was that the Lord had heard my cry and answered my prayer. He had probably given an instruction to an angel to bring it back to me from wherever it was. Glory be to Him!

> I will lift up mine eyes unto the hills, from whence cometh my help.
> My help cometh from the Lord, which made heaven and earth.
>
> Psalm 121:1-2, KJV

As Shining Light Church was growing, we were receiving a lot of visiting ministers. And whenever necessary, I would volunteer to host them in my house. I would drive them wherever they needed to go and would care for them. Many ministers blessed my home in the process.

On 27 June 1998, I invited many friends at home for my birthday celebration. The party was in full swing. We were eating, singing, and praising God. At one point, my landline phone rang. I picked it up in the middle of the festive noise. At first, I could not hear properly. The music was turned down to enable me attend to the phone call. At the end of the receiver, I heard a voice sobbing. My heart sank. As I could not recognize who it was, I asked, "Hello! Who is this?" No answer came, only sobbings. Then I realized that it was the voice of the wife of the SRSG (Special Representative of the Secretary General), my boss at the peacekeeping mission in Luanda, Angola. The voice was faint and trembling.

"Is this Leontine?" She asked.

"Yes," I responded.

She cried louder on the phone. My heart started pounding in my chest. I called her by her name and asked her to tell me what was going on and she said, "I'm calling to inform you that Maitre has died in a plane crash," and then she hung up the phone. Maitre was the nickname the SRSG was known under on the mission field. I screamed and shouted in shock. The party stopped short. I cried bitterly. I cried, and cried, and cried. Later on, I called someone from Angola to find out what had exactly happened. I was told that the SRSG and his team had all perished in the plane crash while on a mission from Togo to Abidjan, Côte d'Ivoire. The team was composed of two pilots, the mission spokesperson, the political advisor, a bodyguard, and some other staff members.

In my anguish and cries to the Lord, the chilling truth dawned on me. If I had decided not to follow God's footsteps and declined the job offer here, I would have stayed in Angola to continue working closely with the SRSG. I probably would have been part of the team that accompanied him on that trip, as was often the case whenever he traveled for official purposes within Luanda and the region. I also would have perished in the plane crash. I cried even more. I measured then the love and grace of God for me. I realized that God had saved and protected my life by asking me to move along with Him. Honor be to Him!

> Mine eyes shall be upon the faithful of the land,
> that they may dwell with me: he that walketh in
> a perfect way, he shall serve me.
>
> Psalm 101: 6, KJV

I asked my office for leave to travel to Côte d'Ivoire where the UN agencies had made arrangements for the remains of the casualties to be prepared for transportation and burial. Then I traveled to Mali, the home country of the SRSG to pay my last respect to him and to all those who perished and present my condolences to the bereaved families.

A month later, I received a letter from the UN Headquarters in New York, indicating that they had agreed to change my entry level from P2 to P3 with back pay of almost a year. It was as if I had left UNAVEM III in Angola with a P3 level to go to ICTR Rwanda as I had wanted. The Lord showed me that I did well to be sensitive to His voice and obey Him. I am so grateful to God, my Father and my provider. He rewarded my obedience in ways I could not have even thought or imagined. This unique experience has showed me how important it is to walk by faith and not by sight. I shared this great testimony in the church and with the ICTR prayer group in Kigali and later on in Arusha, Tanzania. It built up my spirit and strengthened my relationship with God. Once again, the Lord showed himself faithful to me. May His Name be exalted!

> It is better to trust in the Lord than to put confidence in man.
>
> It is better to trust in the Lord than to put confidence in princes.
>
> Psalm 118:8-9, KJV

God's favor was upon me indeed. During the elections organized by the staff association to fill in the various posts, I was elected as the representative of the professional category after competing with many other staff members. The other posts to be filled included president, vice president, treasurer, representative of field service, secretary, deputy secretary, and public relations officer.

The elected president of the staff association and many other colleagues relied on me to draft, because of my language and writing skills, the reports of the staff meetings or the letters to be sent to the ICTR management and/or the UN senior officials at the UN Headquarters in New York on behalf of the ICTR Staff.

FAMILY LIFE

With my new signed contract, I had exceptional benefits which included a contract for a longer duration (two years instead of six months) renewable and payment of an education grant for dependent children. As part of my entitlements, ICTR was to pay for the tickets of my husband and children to enable them to join me at the duty station and travel back abroad for schooling purposes if need be, which it did. This established administrative procedure was referred to as official installation of the staff member's family. My husband and I therefore decided to send our daughters to a boarding school in Lugano, Switzerland, under the education grant scheme. The school was called TASIS (The American School in Switzerland). It was one of the very few US schools located in Europe. Only Eunice, our firstborn, stayed in France with my husband. She was already attending the last year of the high school known in the French education system as *terminale* and was preparing for her international baccalaureate. Diyenat, Maud, and Capucine attended the boarding school for several years, ranging from three to seven, before they would graduate to move to different universities in the United States of America. During those years, my husband and I traveled a great deal to Switzerland to attend parents' meetings or their graduations. During the school holidays, my husband would drive from France to Switzerland via Belgium, Germany, and Luxembourg to pick them up and would drive them back to Switzerland when their schooling resumed. One trip was about nine hundred kilometers.

My daughters liked the boarding school life in TASIS. They were able to settle quickly in that school that was based on the American education system, although they came from a French system. And whenever they came to Kigali, Rwanda, to join me for their summer vacation, they would meet the children of the other UN staff members who were also visiting their parents during the same period and became friends. They also performed extremely well at TASIS. On one graduation ceremony, I remember my daughter Maud received the only Award for Integrity in the whole of TASIS which had over three hundred students from all over the world, and Capucine—known in the school for her outstanding skills in basketball and as the youngest basketball captain—obtained four Most Valuable Players awards.

During my fifth year in Rwanda, I was officially transferred to ICTR in Arusha, Tanzania, to work for the court. My church, friends, and colleagues had organized very moving farewell parties for me on the occasion of my departure. I left Kigali on 29 September 2002.

IN ARUSHA, TANZANIA

IN THE UNITED NATIONS INTERNATIONAL CRIMINAL TRIBUNAL FOR RWANDA (UNICTR)

I joined a larger team of translators and interpreters working for the court. At the same time, I became part of a fellowship called UNICTR Christian Fellowship. It had been started by an ICTR interpreter whom God had inspired and called to serve Him, alongside his spouse; they were Bishop John and Apostle Trice of Zion City Church in Arusha. Bishop John is its spiritual father. They would meet from Monday to Thursday at 1:00 p.m. until 2:00 p.m. I was later appointed as member of the Fellowship Executive Committee, in charge of praise and worship—a responsibility I still assume today. The leaders in the committee were Kate Aboagye as coordinator of the fellowship and later replaced by Pastor Randolph Tebbs; Irma Adjete as spiritual advisor; Tolu Olowoye as secretary; Pastor Moses Mutaasa as treasurer, later replaced by Debra Tulcidas; Christine Ndahura, in charge of the social welfare; Feza Ramazani as deputy praise and worship leader; and Mama Stella Karumuna, Mama Jennifer Kahurananga and a man we nicknamed *Evangelist,* as elders. The fellowship was made up of Christians from various denominations belonging to ICTR and the East African Community as well as local churches in Arusha. It nurtures its members through sermons, Bible studies, prayer and fasting sessions. It organizes prayers for the authorities, the country of Tanzania and other countries, the senior officials of international organizations—especially ICTR and EAC—visits to orphanages and juvenile prisons where its members minister, as well as Christmas carols which were usually attended by ICTR senior officials, staff members, and their families and also invited guests. It became quickly known within the office and in the local community. I have been spiritually fed and blessed through my involvement in the ICTR Christian Fellowship.

I also joined the volleyball and the track teams of ICTR and participated in the UN games—a yearly event organized by all UN agencies.

After ten years of work in international organizations as a French translator-interpreter and another ten years in the UN, the work became routine and I started looking for ways to develop myself. I prayed about it. I went for training to Salamanca, Spain, to improve my knowledge of Spanish and took part in a number of trainings offered in-house by the UN.

One night, while I was watching the news on TV, a documentary showing the tragedy and distress of massively displaced populations in Sudan was being commented. A thought suddenly came to my mind: *Since the UN Secretary General Ban Ki-moon is emphasizing on the need for the United Nations to have a multiskilled mobile staff within its various departments and agencies, you could ask for a lateral move from the Language Section you are presently in to the External Relations and Strategic Planning Section in the ICTR. This would enable you to put to use and develop the diplomatic skills you acquired while working for the Embassy of the Republic of the Congo in Washington, DC.* I was very surprised and happy. *How come such an idea never crossed my mind before?* I acknowledged the Lord right there for that leading of the Spirit and resolved the next day to put that idea into implementation.

The following day, I met my immediate supervisor in the Language Services Section and shared the idea I just had, and she strongly encouraged me. I then wrote an official letter to the chief administrator of the ICTR. God is great! Only two weeks later, I received an official response authorizing my lateral move to the External Relations and Strategic Planning Section (ERSPS), headed by Mr. Roland Kouassi Amoussouga, senior legal adviser, and ICTR spokesperson. In that section, I was appointed protocol and external relations officer in charge of the protocol and conferences services unit. I had, under my supervision, a protocol assistant and was also the coordinator of all ERSPS interns.

I assumed the new duties of protocol and external relations officer from October 2007 until September 2012. They gave me considerable exposure and visibility. I worked closely and came into contact with the ICTR senior officials: the President, the Prosecutor, and the Registrar; high profile dignitaries from the UN Headquarters including the Secretary General, the Under-Secretary General for legal affairs, the Under-Secretary General for human resource management; the heads of the UN agencies, such as the United Nations Educational, Scientific and Cultural Organization (UNESCO), the United Nations Development Programme (UNDP), the United Nations Economic Commission for Africa (UNECA), just to mention a few; members of the Diplomatic Corps; the Tanzanian government and local authorities; the Rwandan authorities; other government representatives, as well as heads of international organizations and various institutions.

My work was demanding, but also rewarding. It was highly appreciated by the ICTR management. May I, at this stage, mention and commend, in particular, my immediate supervisor and first reporting officer, the chief of ERSPS, Mr. Roland Amoussouga, who believed in me and taught me, by example, the nitty-gritty of the protocol profession, international cooperation and communication, as well as my second reporting officer, the registrar of the tribunal, Mr. Adama Dieng, Assistant-Secretary General of the United Nations, who trusted me and my skills and gave me the opportunity to perform at that level.

Here again, the Lord was gracious and faithful. He gave me favor and breakthrough. While many other colleagues had also requested lateral transfers to other sections and did not succeed, my request was not only processed within a few days but was also considered favorably. Blessed be the Lord Almighty!

> Seest thou a man diligent in his business? He shall stand before kings; he shall not stand before mean men.
>
> Proverbs 22:29, KJV

Meanwhile, the International Criminal Tribunal for Rwanda had come to the end of its mandate and had greatly downsized. The large majority of its staff had left and some of its functions had already been transferred to the Mechanism for International Criminal Tribunals (MICT) that started operations in July 2012.

IN THE LOCAL CHURCH

I also became a member a local church called Bethel World Outreach church, a branch of Bethel World Outreach Ministries—the Church I attended while in the United States. In Bethel Arusha, I served as a praise and worship leader, an elder and a board member. When my husband joined me in Arusha, the pastor, later on, appointed him as an elder in charge of the building project of the church because of his architectural background. Bethel had a very small congregation of less than a hundred members and those attending the church regularly were about twenty to forty. We had been serving and ministering in Bethel for three years when the church started experiencing problems in the areas of spiritual and physical growth, human resources and finance. Some disagreements arose on how the church was being run and on how its finances were being spent. The three pastors of the board, the senior pastor and I reviewed the situation and made some recommendations. And along with the congregation, we started praying about it.

It was over that period that I had two dreams which were a week apart. The church members were meeting under a shed with iron sheet roofs and no walls, which was then upgraded into a tent. In my first dream, I saw the senior pastor announcing to the whole congregation gathered that he was to minister at a funeral outside the church in some village. He was inviting the church members to come along, especially the board members. We were all supposed to meet at a certain location to walk as a group to the said village, but at the appointed time, only a few had arrived. We decided to wait a little longer for the others, especially the senior pastor and his spouse. The church members trickled in and by the time we started to walk to the village, it was rather late. On the way, people started to quarrel. Some were wondering why, as a church, people were behaving that way; some were trying to explain the said behavior. By the time we reached the village, the burial had already taken place, and the senior pastor was not present. Then I woke up. I prayed about it and kept the dream to myself.

A week later, I had a second dream. I found myself under the rectangular church tent where we had our services, as it was raining heavily outside. As the water started flooding in, I tried to block the loopholes where the water was entering inside the tent in an attempt to minimize the flooding. I was screaming, "Help, help!" Then I saw my senior pastor behind me. He was talking with one of the church's workers. He did not hear my cry for help and did not seem to know that there was a heavy rain outside and that the tent was being flooded. At one point, the water became too much for me to bear. In my panic, I brutally woke up.

I told my husband about both dreams. He thought it would be good to share them with the senior pastor, his spouse, and the other board members, so that we could pray together. And I did so. By this time, the disagreements and complaints in the church about this had become frequent and visible. The atmosphere in the church deteriorated. Some church members left and did not return. I remember a particular lady who, on a few occasions, gave prophecies during the church service; she was told to keep quiet and eventually left.

One night, I was reading the Word and praying for my church, my family and relatives, especially those who were not yet saved. While I was praying, the Holy Spirit impressed upon me to read a Bible passage. It was Ezekiel 34:1–10, KJV.

And the word of the Lord came unto me, saying,

Son of man, prophesy against the shepherds of Israel, prophesy, and say unto them, Thus saith the Lord God unto the shepherds; Woe be to the shepherds of Israel that do feed themselves! Should not the shepherds feed the flocks?

Ye eat the fat, and ye clothe you with the wool, ye kill them that are fed: but ye feed not the flock.

The diseased have ye not strengthened, neither have ye healed that which was sick, neither have ye bound up that which was broken, neither have ye brought again that which was driven away, neither have ye sought that which was lost; but with force and with cruelty have ye ruled them.

And they were scattered, because there is no shepherd: and they became meat to all the beasts of the field, when they were scattered.

My sheep wandered through all the mountains, and upon every high hill: yea, my flock was scattered upon all the face of the earth, and none did search or seek after them.

Therefore, ye shepherds, hear the word of the Lord;

As I live, saith the Lord God, surely because my flock became a prey, and my flock became meat to every beast of the field, because there was no shepherd, neither did my shepherds search for my flock, but the shepherds fed themselves, and fed not my flock;

Therefore, O ye shepherds, hear the word of the Lord;

Thus saith the Lord God; Behold, I am against the shepherds; and I will require my flock at their hand, and cause them to cease from feeding the flock; neither shall the shepherds feed themselves any more; for I will deliver my flock from their mouth, that they may not be meat for them.

As I read, the meaning of every single word was revealed to me. At the end, the whole picture terrified me. I was filled with apprehension for the fate of the church. I prayed and decided the next morning to share this revelation with our church leaders.

Unfortunately, the revelation was not taken seriously. A few months later, the church gradually dwindled and died. The senior pastor resigned from Bethel World Outreach Ministries. The congregation was scattered. It was a painful experience.

My husband and I stayed in Bethel for five years. Although we knew a few churches around, we prayed and asked God to show us where to go to serve Him. One Sunday, in 2008, a Christian couple who used to attend our home fellowship invited us to their church. It was unknown to us and happened to be very close to our house. The church was called Dominion Restoration Church and had over five hundred members. We attended the church service and felt peaceful and comfortable. My husband and I eventually joined the church as full-fledged members. Both of us are still serving the Lord in that church as elders, among others, assisting our Pastor Charles Akwera and his spouse, Judith Akwera, in whatever capacities they deemed it necessary, be it as leaders in charge of the Youth or in charge of Protocol and the Ushers. As our spiritual fathers, Pastor Charles and Mama Muchungaji Judith have been a real blessing to my family. Working for the Kingdom of God under their leadership has been uplifting and rewarding, despite the challenges. We are happy. We appreciate God for having taken us there and given us the opportunity to join the other laborers in his field. Praise be to His name!

The Bethel pastor in one of the remote branches of Bethel World Outreach Church contacted me and my husband and the other three pastors who were sitting on the Bethel board. We were all UN and EAC staff members. His name was Pastor Baltazar. He asked us to work with him and support the church. So, once a month, or depending on our availability, we took turns to go and ministered there during church services and seminars. We also supported that branch financially. It had over three hundred members and was doing well. We still support it.

AT HOME

I started a home fellowship with one sister in Christ, Margaret Mwaura. We would meet at my house on Thursday evenings. The fellowship had grown and was composed of about ten families of various nationalities, including the families of Margaret Mwaura, Irma Adjete, Pastors Peggy and Randolph Tebbs, Doreen Maina, Debra Tulcidas, Alphonse Van, Forias and Renifa Madenga, Arlette Bikok, Pastor Mayunga, the late brother Moses and Esther Mutwaliza, and ourselves, the Mabikas. The said families were from Kenya, Togo, USA, Liberia, Tanzania, Zimbababwe, Côte d'Ivoire, Cameroon, and Congo-Brazzaville. We have rendered to God powerful praise and worship sessions, thanksgivings, shared the Word of God, prayed and fasted for our nations, our churches, our employers, families, relatives, friends, and the Saints. The Lord has performed many miracles in our midst and answered innumerable prayers. These families were prayer partners and had mutually edified and supported one another. May God bless them mightily!

> "Behold, how good and how pleasant it is for brethren to dwell together in unity!"
>
> Psalm 133:1, KJV

INVOLVEMENT IN OTHER CHRISTIAN MINISTRIES

We supported a ministry that our brethren, Kate and Alex Aboagye from Ghana, started in Arusha called Family Life Seminar. The purpose of the ministry was to empower families by tackling family concerns such as marriage foundations, seasons of life including singlehood and widowhood, divorce, parenting, stewardship, communication and conflict resolution in the home. Alongside other persons, we assisted Kate in the planning, organizing, and unfolding of international seminars on family issues. When Kate, who was also a staff member of the United Nations International Criminal Tribunal for Rwanda, was transferred from Arusha, the headquarters, to the suboffice in The Hague, she organized a small gathering at her house. All those who supported her in the ministry were in attendance. It was then that Mr. and Mrs. Aboagye, in their farewell statement, announced that the Lord had spoken to them to put my husband and I in charge of the Family Life Seminar ministry after them. This came as a surprise to us as we were still beginners in the ministry. Amazed at God's ways, my husband and I accepted this responsibility. We were therefore officially designated as their successors. They spoke words of encouragement and prayed for us. This occurred in 2005, two years after the ministry began in Arusha.

During the first year in the leadership of the ministry, my husband and I consulted some Christian brethren to form the organizing committee of the Family Life Seminar ministry. The said committee was composed of the following: Jennifer Karegyesa, Beth Luzuka, Pastors Peggy and Randolph Tebbs, Pastor Stephen and Mary Owino, Pastor Robert and Christine, Pastor Mayunga, as well as Leontine and Pascal Mabika.

Over the past seven years as coordinators of the Family Life Seminar ministry in Arusha, the committee had organized an annual international seminar. The topics had included: role modeling as spouse, widow, and youth, parenting, the marriage dance, etc. The guest speakers at these seminars had been our mentors. They were Reverend Ken and Joy Kimiywe, senior pastor, singer, and overseer of women ministry, Nairobi Pentecostal Church (NPC), Valley Road, Nairobi; Dr. Jayne and David Mutiga, professor at the University of Nairobi and engineer, elders in NPC; Mary and Kirabo Lukwago, owners of a Christian bookstore called the New Day; David and Margaret, marriage counselors; Ben Benson, marriage counselor; and Alex and Kate Aboagye, founders of Arusha Family Life Seminar Ministry. They had trained us and some other members of the organizing committee in marriage counseling and family issues. These seminars had individually gathered up to 150 participants and imparted positively on many families in Arusha. We have testimonies of changed family lives from participants of the seminars. I would like here to extend our heartfelt appreciation to our mentors for teaching and guiding us in this ministry and to the organizing committee and Family Life partners for having believed in us, and for supporting us in this ministry through counsels, prayers, material, and financial assistance. May the Lord richly bless you!

> "Therefore, my beloved brethren, be ye stedfast, unmoveable, always abounding in the work of the Lord, forasmuch as ye know that your labour is not in vain in the Lord."
>
> 1 Corinthians 15:58, KJV

HOW GOD HAS TRANSFORMED MY LIFE

I am pleased to mention under this chapter instances where the inner voice materialized God's leading in my life. I am convinced that the Lord can speak to us to prepare for the unfolding of certain events. However, being human, we tend not to pay attention:

- The UN management had appointed me within UNICTR as member of the Central Review Panel (CRP), a recruitment and promotion body for the general service staff. Many other colleagues were also appointed. The chief of personnel called a meeting for all of the appointees to explain the purpose and the duties involved in sitting on the CRP. About ten minutes before the appointed time, I was in my office getting ready to leave for the meeting when very unexpectedly, I heard a soft voice speak to my ear, "Prepare to go and chair the meeting." In response to the voice, I said to myself, "Chair the meeting? What do you mean to chair the meeting? The chief of personnel is officially chairing the meeting!" I grabbed my writing pad and my pen and off I went to the meeting venue. In the room, there were about thirty participants including the chief of administration and the chief of personnel. After their welcoming remarks, the two officials explained to us the purpose of the meeting and underlined the importance of the Central Review Panel within the UNICTR. The CRP mandate was to review the procedure for recruiting or promoting the general service staff as followed by human resources (HR) and make appropriate recommendations to the UNICTR management for final approval. The chief of personnel indicated that the Central Review Panel was required to have a small committee to lead it, composed of a chairperson, a secretary and three substantive members, with alternate members replacing them in case of absence. And the incumbent of these positions would have to be elected right there by the attendees, except the two officials. He first asked if there's anyone who would like to volunteer for the position of chairperson of the committee. One person raised his hand. Then he asked for written nominations for the same position. The name of the volunteer and the nominees were jotted down. And the same went for the other four positions on the committee. Then time for election came. Anonymous ballots were taken.

Surprisingly enough, I won as the chairperson. I did not expect to win because among the competitors, there were people who were senior than me, both in age and in grade. When all the positions were filled, the chief of personnel initiated a round of applause for the elected members and said, "It is now my pleasure to request the newly elected chairperson to take over and chair the meeting." It was then that the soft voice spoke quickly to me again saying, "I told you!" I remembered what it had told me earlier in my office about being ready to go and chair the meeting. I was thrilled in my spirit. My heart was pounding in my chest. In my heart, I quickly asked the Lord to forgive me and to guide me in the conduct of the deliberations. I did not know where to start from. The Lord was faithful. The term of office on the Central Review Panel was two years. I chaired the panel for four consecutive years. I would like to appreciate the Lord for giving me patience, a word of wisdom, and the ability to reach consensus, especially at times when matters became controversial within the CRP. It was a real school of learning!

Sometime in May 2010, my husband and I were invited by our former pastors in Rwanda to go to Kigali and help them with the architectural plans of the church they wanted to build on the land they had bought. During our three-day visit in Kigali, Rwanda, the Lord spoke to me one night in our hotel room. It was on Sunday, 23 May 2010 at 2:45 a.m. My husband was sleeping next to me. I suddenly woke up. I went to the bathroom and then back to bed, but I could not sleep anymore. I tossed and turned in bed in an attempt to go back to sleep. Nothing. Suddenly, an inner voice spoke to me, "Why don't you read your Bible in the meantime?" As quietly as possible to avoid waking up my husband, I took my Bible from the night table where I had placed it and put on the bedside light. As I opened it, my eyes fell on the book of Matthew, chapter seven. I started reading from verse one. As I did so, certain verses were being highlighted under my eyes with a certain light, as if with a torchlight, to draw my attention onto them in particular. The funny thing was that the meaning of those passages was also being shown to me. Then the inner voice spoke to me again and said, "Get up and go to your computer to write down whatever you are hearing in order to share it with your daughters and the other youth." I obeyed and wrote down the message below:

1. Covenant

I would like, first of all, said the Lord, to remind you of the covenant we have between us (As Mabika Family on 31 August 1998 in Kigali; we concluded a covenant with the Lord, the terms of which are as below).

> But this shall be the covenant that I will make with the house of Israel; After those days, saith the Lord, I will put my law in their inward parts, and write it

in their hearts; and will be their God, and they shall be my people.

> Jeremiah 31:33, KJV

You asked me in line with that covenant to:

a. Enable you to consecrate your lives to God.

> Neither yield ye your members as instruments of unrighteousness unto sin: but yield yourselves unto God, as those that are alive from the dead, and your members as instruments of righteousness unto God.
>
> Romans 6:13, KJV

b. Make you sensitive to the voice of the Lord.

> And thine ears shall hear a word behind thee, saying, This is the way, walk ye in it, when ye turn to the right hand, and when ye turn to the left.
>
> Isaiah 30:21, KJV

c. Give you the fruit of the Spirit.

> But the fruit of the Spirit is love, joy, peace, longsuffering, gentleness, goodness, faith; meekness, temperance: against such there is no law.
>
> Galatians 5:22–23, KJV

d. Protect you against the wiles and schemes of Satan.

> Put on the whole armor of God, that ye may be able to stand against the wiles of the devil.
>
> Ephesians 6:11, KJV

e. Make you the head and not the tail in whatever you do.

> And the Lord shall make thee the head, and not the tail; and thou shalt be above only, and thou shalt not be beneath; if that thou hearken unto the commandments of the Lord thy God, which I command thee this day, to observe and to do them:
>
> Deuteronomy 28:13, KJV

f. Give you strength to live by this covenant.

> But they that wait upon the Lord shall renew their strength; they shall mount up with wings as eagles; they shall run, and not be weary; and they shall walk, and not faint.
>
> Isaiah 40:31, KJV

I am the God of one word, and my words remain forever; I have been with you and I continue to be. Each one of you has tasted my faithfulness and sometimes, testified about it. It is with this in mind that I would like you to convey to your daughters and the other youth my following words.

2. First Message

> Give not that which is holy unto the dogs, neither cast ye your pearls before swine, lest they trample them under their feet, and turn again and rend you.
>
> Matthew 7:6, KJV

Believe it when you say you are the apple of my eye; my Son was given in ransom for you. He redeemed you on the cross, with his blood. You are precious to me! The Word I put in your heart since you started on this earth is there to guide you and make you live by it. It is like jewellery which adorns you and makes you look beautiful; Do not play with your lives which are sacred to me and give them to the dogs to play with like toys; the precious gifts (the pearls) I have entrusted with you, do not give them to the pigs, considered to be impure, unfit for God, a place where demons when chased by the Spirit of God, go and hide. You are called to have dominion over dogs and pigs, but not to live with them; You are called to live with men of your kind, who are like you, and not with those who are unlike you (the dogs and pigs who would not appreciate your value because they are just "animals," with no soul, no spirit as Christ is not in them, and therefore walk on you to kill you (your soul and Spirit). The body goes back to the earth when it dies and does not really matter.

3. Second Message

> Enter ye in at the strait gate: for wide is the gate, and broad is the way, that leadeth to destruction, and many there be which go in thereat:
>
> Because strait is the gate, and narrow is the way, which leadeth unto life, and few there be that find it.
>
> Matthew 7:13–14, KJV

Do not live like the people of this world; do not conform to this world; live like kings and queens who fully know that they have a kingdom as their home, which they will go to when time comes, and that living on this earth is just temporary; but as Ambassadors of Christ who live according to the rules and regulations of God the Father, God the Son and God the Holy Spirit; you are called to change this stiff-necked generation that is massively living according to the standards of this world and therefore miss heaven. The gate to hell is wider and wider because many, willingly (because they have chosen not to heed the voice of God) or unwillingly (because deceived by Satan) are walking through it to their death; A few young people like yourselves know me; so only few will follow me and will find the gate which leads to eternal life; Let your salvation make a difference in this generation!

4. Third Message

> Not every one that saith unto me, Lord, Lord, shall enter into the kingdom of heaven; but he that doeth the will of my Father which is in heaven.
>
> Matthew 7:21, KJV

Those who truly know me are those who obey me, who are doers of my Word. Obedience is better than sacrifice; You may know me and confess me with your lips, but not from your heart where the Word of God is fed and kept to guide you in life. When I say in 2Cor 6:14-16, KJV

> "Be ye not unequally yoked together with unbelievers: for what fellowship hath righteousness with unrighteousness? And what communion hath light with darkness?
>
> And what concord hath Christ with Belial? Or what part hath he that believeth with an infidel?
>
> And what agreement hath the temple of God with idols? For ye are the temple of the living God; as God hath said, I will dwell in them, and walk in them; and I will be their God, and they shall be my people.

I know what my word creates when I speak. I also know what it creates when it is disobeyed. This is why I say I am the Alpha and the Omega, the beginning and the end; I speak of the end because I can see the beginning. Obey my word! Do not reason it! A tree is known by its fruit!

5. Fourth Message

> Therefore whosoever heareth these sayings of mine, and doeth them, I will liken him unto a wise man, which built his house upon a rock:
>
> And the rain descended, and the floods came, and the winds blew, and beat upon that house; and it fell not: for it was founded upon a rock.
>
> And every one that heareth these sayings of mine, and doeth them not, shall be likened unto a foolish man, which built his house upon the sand:
>
> And the rain descended, and the floods came, and the winds blew, and beat upon that house; and it fell: and great was the fall of it.
>
> Matthew 7:24–27, KJV

Live wisely and not foolishly! Read the story of the wise and foolish virgins who were waiting for their master to come. See those who were prepared and those who were not and why they were not prepared. You all desire to build a house of your own. Therefore, use material which comes from heaven, with labourers from the kingdom, using the foundation that was laid long ago and that already exists: Christ, Jesus! When trial comes, it will not fall down. It will stand because of the strength of the foundation. You will live in a proper house, the one I have always purposed for you, not the one that you built with your own hands, your own materials and your own workers. Build your houses with me!

- I shared the above message with my daughters. In August of the same year, the Spirit led me to organize a youth seminar for singles and bachelors in Arusha in order to share that message and speak to them about God's purposes for their lives. My husband and I prayed about it. The Lord gave me inspiration as to the program and the various topics to be discussed during that seminar. We contacted four other couples. They agreed to support us and be the guest speakers at the seminar. All the speakers were from Cameroon, Liberia, Nigeria, Uganda, Tanzania, and Congo-Brazzaville. The venue of the seminar was a church sanctuary we had rented for the occasion. A total of three hundred young men and women, the full capacity of the church sanctuary, turned up despite many other events which were taking place in the same city at the same time, such as university graduation, the UN family fun day, and a trade fair. It rained only over the church in that area that day! Many youth testimonials were recorded, saying they were blessed. What a miracle! Two days later, we rendered a thanksgiving to the Lord.

In March of 2012, a second youth seminar was organized. The Lord manifested his presence in a powerful way. A youth bureau for Arusha was elected by the two hundred and eighty participants present. It was composed of the president, the vice president, the secretary, the deputy secretary, and the prayer coordinator with whom we are working today.

- A prophet from Iceland named Kolbein came to Arusha, Tanzania, to minister at the invitation of pastor Sylvain from the Democratic Republic of Congo. It was in the context of an indoor crusade. A good number of people attended. Two things happened to me during that crusade. Firstly, among the crowd, the prophet called some people and gave them prophecies according to the leading of the Spirit in him. My husband and I were called to the stage to be prayed for. He spoke to us in these terms, "You've passed the test, I am pleased with you! I've given you a new name. You are now called Abraham and Sarah. You will bear many children!" Then the prophet anointed us with oil. My husband and I were amazed at the prophecy and we felt as if we were flying. We thanked the Lord and returned home, wondering what the Lord meant. The next day, in the afternoon session of the crusade, the praise and worship was in full swing. My heart was full of joy. I was suddenly carried into the spirit, while in the physical, my body was dancing and swinging in circles. My husband wondered what was happening to me. In the spirit, I saw the following scene unfold before my eyes: I was watching from above as if I was hanging high in the air. There were so many people standing in one line close to each other in a rectangular room. The strange thing was that they all looked the same and had the same smile on their faces. On the right side, there were three people sitting on chairs under a shade. Although I could not distinguish their faces, I immediately understood that these people were very important. Inside the rectangular room, I saw three people dancing while holding flags and large round circles as if they were performing rhythmic gymnastics before the three dignitaries. All of a sudden, I saw myself in the middle of the rectangular room. I was looking at the people around and they were not talking. Yet, I could hear their voices cheering me on, "Go Leontine, go! Go Leontine, go!" Then I heard a soft voice coming from above me and it said. "Leontine, get your flag!" Out of nowhere, a flag came into my right hand. And joyfully, I started dancing, swinging, and jumping left and right before the three VIPs. I could form circles and various figures with my body as if I had no bones. I had become very flexible. I was happy and smiling. I was performing alone inside the rectangular room. I was still hearing the cheers. At one point, I felt the eyes of the VIP sitting in the middle looking at me intently. I could not look at his eyes. All of a sudden, I saw him extend his right hand toward my face and almost covering it. Then I felt hot air being blown in my face as if I was a balloon. My whole body, arms, legs, and feet were being inflated. I felt some pain as my body was being stretched out beyond its limits. I could see my whole body floating in the air like the *petit bonhomme Michelin*. When my body was full of hot air, the hand moved away from my face and the supply of hot air was cut off instantly. As my body was floating in the air, I could see from above three people from the crusade hall touching my body and trying to hold me so I could not move. I said to myself, "Why are they touching me? They should not touch my body!" Suddenly, I found myself back in the crusade hall where the praise and worship session was just ending. The surrounding noise hit me. I opened my eyes and saw the faces of my husband and Sister Tolulope and Pastor Tebbs looking at me. My husband was holding me tightly in his arms. I wondered what the problem was. They later on explained to me that they had been seeing my body in the physical dancing, jumping and forming incredible figures and that, at one point, I had put my hands on my stomach as if I was in pain. They had to hold me to prevent me from falling down. I then realized that what I was experiencing in the spirit was actually being manifested in the physical. During the testimony time, I was invited to share with the congregation the vision I had had during the crusade. Prophet Kolbein told the congregation that the Lord had allowed me to see the third heaven. He indicated that the Lord had given my husband and I a prophecy and that He had not done this for nothing. He added that this couple would experience something and that everyone would hear about it.

- God confirmed all this in a miraculous way. In September of 2009, my husband and I went to France for our home leave. A couple friend of ours named Pierre and Laurence Spataro invited us. We had planned to visit them for a weekend as we had not met, nor spoken for more than six years. They were wonderful man and woman of God. My husband and I were excited when we took the trip. Pierre had called on our mobile to inform us that he would be slightly late in picking us up as there was a lot of traffic on the way. My husband and I came out of the arrival area of the railway station and sat outside waiting for him. A few minutes later, we heard his voice, welcoming us in these terms, "We are very much excited. Sarah and Abraham are visiting us today!" My husband and I turned our faces where the voice was coming from and we saw Pierre with his arms wide open, running to embrace and welcome us. My husband and I were shocked when we heard him call us "Sarah and Abraham." We had not shared with him the prophecy of Prophet Kolbein. We understood this as a confirmation of that prophecy. We spent a quality time with our friends Pierre and Laurence and their daughter Sarah, sharing testimonies of our lives and praising God. We visited them a couple of times after that.

- Another experience through which the Lord confirmed the aforesaid prophecy was the following: my husband and I and our four daughters had agreed to travel to Israel in 2010 to spend Christmas there and visit the Holy Land together. Two of our children were living in the United Sates. One was studying in the university and the other one working. Our firstborn was working in Dublin, Ireland. The third one was preparing an MBA at ESAMI (Eastern and Southern African Management Institute) in Arusha, Tanzania and was living with us. A week before we took the trip to Tel Aviv in Israel, our daughter Eunice called us on Skype to share something with us. She said she had fasted and prayed to God and believed in him so she could find school fees for her MBA. "Mom, I had a revelation I'd like to share with you. While I was praying, the Lord revealed to me a number of things about each one of us in the family," she said. "What did He say?" I inquired. She indicated that she had a message for each one of us. May I share with you what she said about her father as the testimony concerns him mostly? She said the Lord told her, "I'm going to make your dad a new man." And then, she saw her dad in a vision, preaching to a crowd, laying hands on people, and people were getting healed. And she said, "Mom, I didn't understand that vision. However, it came to me so vividly!" My husband and I were listening to her and following her on Skype. On 21 December 2010, we all gathered in Metropolitan Hotel in Tel Aviv after taking different flights. On 22 December, my husband organized a family prayer session in order to put the guided tour in the hands of God. We prayed as a family and appreciated God for the opportunity to spend Christmas together again; the last time was in 2000. We had been in different locations—some in Africa, some in Europe, and some in the United States of America. On 23 December, we visited various Christian sites, including Mount of Olives, Canaan, Nazareth, the village of Mary Magdalene, the Garden of Gethsemane, and many other places. We went to the Jordan River to rededicate our lives to Christ as we had already been baptized in the water. My husband went into the river and dipped himself into it. He called me and plunged me into the water. He did the same with his lastborn Capucine. When he came out of the water to get his second daughter Diyenat, he slipped and sat flat on the floor with his feet stretched. His eyes were staring at something in the sky and he could not respond to my queries. He started vomiting and then fainted. My husband was rushed to the nearest hospital and was found with a brain hemorrhage due to a ruptured aneurysm. Then he was rushed to Rambam Hospital in Haifa for surgery. He went through two consecutive neurosurgical operations on 24 December 2010. On 26 December, my husband fell into coma. We experienced the darkest hour of our lives; and worst still, it was in a foreign land. I cannot find words to describe it. My daughters and I went before the Lord in prayer and fasting. The Lord literally led us into what to do. By his grace and his mercy, my husband was brought back to life on 4 January 2011 with a message from the Lord. All these miracles are well described in my other book as well as in my husband's book on this particular experience. Many people including medical doctors called my husband the "resurrected one" or "the miracle." According to the statistics given to us by a neurosurgeon, out of a hundred people who have a ruptured aneurysm, half of them died on their way to the hospital. Out of the fifty left, one-third would die while being operated on, one-third would recover but with a lot of disabilities, and the rest would recover properly and my husband was one of them. A thanksgiving ceremony was organized on 25 June 2011 in Arusha before a large audience of about two hundred people, including church ministers, leaders, Christians, Muslims, and unbelievers. This unique experience has made my family known in Arusha and has transformed our lives as a family.

CONCLUSION

By sharing my life and these testimonies with you, my intention was to show that God, not only exists, but also takes care of His people. As He indicated in His Word, He can bless the righteous and their descendants up to a thousand generations for those who walk with Him. Although my life, like that of many other human beings, has its ups and downs, I can state with confidence that God has blessed me and my family and continues to do so. I would like, in my turn, to be a blessing, not only to the church of God, but also to the people God brings my way.

The dreams and other experiences in my life have strengthened my faith and demonstrated God's desire to take care of his own people and give them a blessed life while on this earth. I have come to realize how important it is to give to God and His church for the advancement of God's kingdom on earth. None of us can outgive God. I have learned that when we give to God, He gives it back to us "good measure, pressed down, and shaken together, and running over, shall men give into your bosom" (Luke 6:38, KJV).

I am deeply convinced that because I, faithfully and sacrificially, gave to my church and redeemed my pledge in the acquisition of the land of our church—Bethel World Outreach Ministries—in the United States of America, and this, despite my financial duress, the Lord has multiplied my income by almost ten by giving me a UN job, first for three months, and then for the next sixteen years up to the time of writing this book.

I have also realized how important it is to follow the leading of the Spirit—the inner small voice in our heart; the green or red light in us which indicates whether we have to continue with a certain action or not. There were instances when I had not followed these promptings and have regretted it because of the consequences I suffered.

The Lord has settled me in leadership positions, wherever I go, be it at the workplace or in the church. I am always chosen to assume leadership roles and sometimes being appointed even when I am not present. I have also noticed the same trend developing in my daughters' lives.

I would like to sing to the Lord with David in Psalm 138:1–3 (KJV).

> I will praise thee with my whole heart: before the gods will I sing praise unto thee.

> I will worship toward thy holy temple, and praise thy name for thy lovingkindness and for thy truth: for thou hast magnified thy word above all thy name.
>
> In the day when I cried thou answeredst me, and strengthenedst me with strength in my soul.

The Lord has given me new songs, which my husband and I have recorded recently with the assistance of some friends. The title of the album is *Lamb of God*.

As you read these pages, my strongest desire is to encourage you to get to know the Lord and let Him be the Redeemer and Savior of your life in order to give meaning to your life. If you have been saved by confessing the Lord as your personal savior, I would encourage you to maintain the right course and develop a close relationship with Him so that you can have Him led you when necessary. If you have backslidden and your walk with the Lord is not as straight as it ought to be, I beg you to return to your first love and rediscover Him. If you do not yet know our wonderful God, may I urge you to say the following prayer to invite God into your heart and life: "Dear God, I do not know you. I would like to know you and invite you in my life. Come into my heart and lead me. In the mighty name of Jesus I have prayed, Amen!"

With love,
Leontine Birangui Mabika

www.ingramcontent.com/pod-product-compliance
Lightning Source LLC
Chambersburg PA
CBHW020127130526
44591CB00032B/557